Thank You!

Dear Reader,

 Welcome to **"50 Bible Verses to Know My Favorite ABC - Grasping God's Word - 4th Edition Book"**! As an author, I am thrilled to embark on this journey with you and your little ones, unlocking the treasures hidden within the sacred pages of the Holy Bible!

 In this book, your children will discover the 50 most famous Bible verses, from both Old and New Testament. I shortly explained each verse for them to understand further the true meaning of it. My goal is to make the Bible a beloved part of your child's life by using engaging descriptions and beautiful illustrations.

 This book is more than just a collection of verses; it is a captivating adventure that will introduce your children to the extraordinary lessons from the Bible in a way that resonates with their youthful spirits.

 Let's teach your children the beauty and significance of this sacred text, guiding them with love, faith, and compassion. Let the adventure begin!

Adrian Barbu

I dedicate this book to my two children, Vlad and Giulia, who hold an irreplaceable place in my heart

Pixi Story

www.PixiStory.com

In the beginning, God created the Heavens and the Earth

Imagine the most magnificent magic show you can think of, where God appears as the grandest magician of all. He says, "Ta-da!" and creates the sky, the ground, and everything around us in an instant. The twinkling stars, fluffy clouds, and green grass just appear out of thin air, as if by magic!

Honor your father and mother so that you may live long in the land the Lord your God is giving you

Here's a golden rule from God: when you show respect and love to your mom and dad, it's like a secret to having a long and happy life in the amazing world that God has given you, so be a super-duper good kid to them!

Taste and see that the Lord is good; blessed is the one who takes refuge in Him

It's like tasting the most delicious ice cream and realizing that God is even better. So, if you trust in Him and make Him your safe place, you'll have a very happy and life!

EXODUS 20:3

You shall have no other gods before me

God is like the superhero of all, and He wants us to know that we should always, always, put Him first and not let anything else become more important in our hearts, like making sure He's the number one superstar in our lives!

EXODUS 20:15

You shall not steal

Okay, little buddy, here's the deal: God says it's a big no-no to take things that don't belong to you, because it's like being a sneaky pirate, and God wants us to be honest and kind to everyone, so remember, no swiping stuff, it's all about sharing and caring!

The heavens declare the glory of God; the skies proclaim the work of His hands

Hey there, little explorer, when you look up at the big, beautiful sky with all those twinkling stars and fluffy clouds, it's like God's way of saying, 'Look how awesome I am!' because everything up there and all around us shows how amazing and creative God is, just like a gigantic, never-ending art show!

PSALM 118:24

This is the day the Lord has made; let us rejoice and be glad in it

Think of every day as a shiny new toy from God, meant to be enjoyed and celebrated!

The grass withers and the flowers fall, but the word of our God endures forever

Hey, little nature lover, even though the grass gets all droopy and the flowers lose their petals and go 'bye-bye,' God's special words are like a super-strong tree that never, ever goes away, so we can always count on them, like having a forever friend who's always there for us!

But those who hope in the Lord will renew their strength They will soar on wings like eagles

When we trust and believe in God, it's like getting a superpower – we can fly high like majestic eagles, run as fast as race cars without getting tired because God gives us the strength to do amazing things when we put our hope in Him!

So do not fear, for I am with you; do not be dismayed, for I am your God. I will strengthen you and help you

Hey there, little champ, when tough times come knocking at your door, remember that God's got your back, and it's like having a superhero by your side, saying, 'Don't be scared, I'm here for you, and I'll give you all the power to be strong and brave, like holding your hand and never letting go!'

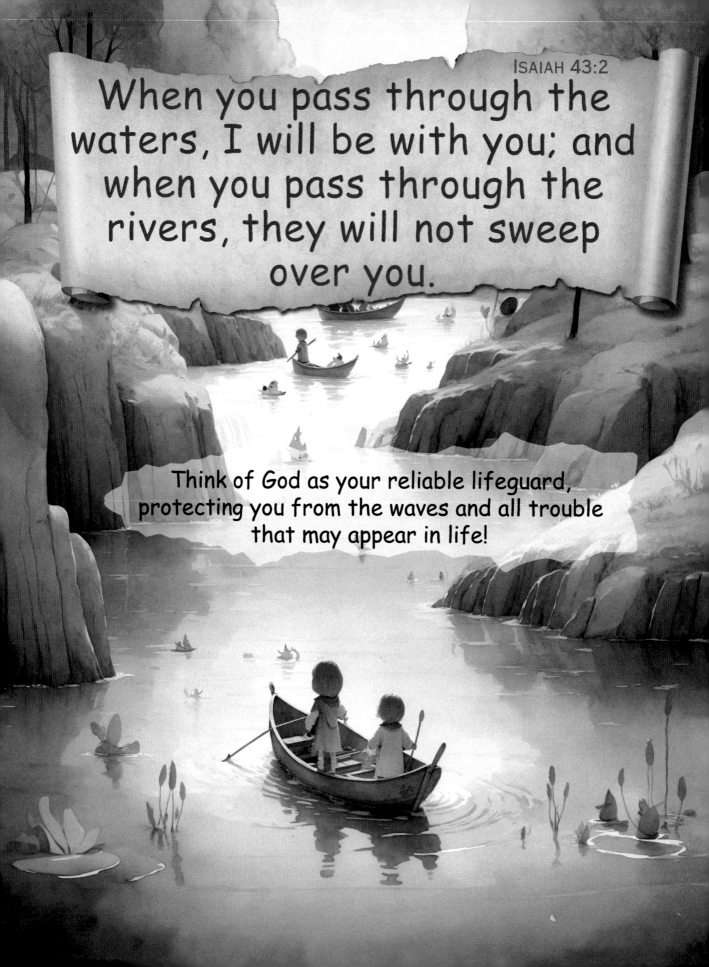

ISAIAH 43:2

When you pass through the waters, I will be with you; and when you pass through the rivers, they will not sweep over you.

Think of God as your reliable lifeguard, protecting you from the waves and all trouble that may appear in life!

1 SAMUEL 16:7

The Lord does not look at the things people look at. People look at the outward appearance, but the Lord looks at the heart

When people see each other, they often judge based on appearance (what clothes they wear for example), but God looks beyond that and sees the goodness in your heart, which is what truly matters to Him!

As for God, His way is perfect: The Lord's word is flawless; He shields all who take refuge in Him

Hey there, little explorer, it's like God has the most amazing GPS ever, and His way of doing things is always just right, His words are like perfect treasure maps that never lead you astray, and when you snuggle up in His loving arms, it's like being in the coziest, strongest fortress where nothing can harm you!

Have I not commanded you? Be strong and courageous. Do not be afraid; do not be discouraged, for the Lord your God will be with you wherever you go

Hey, little champion, it's like God giving you a big pep talk, saying, 'You've got this! Be brave and strong, don't let fear or discouragement stop you, because I'll be right there with you, no matter where you go, like your ultimate, never-leave-your-side best friend!'

The Lord gave, and the Lord has taken away; blessed be the name of the Lord

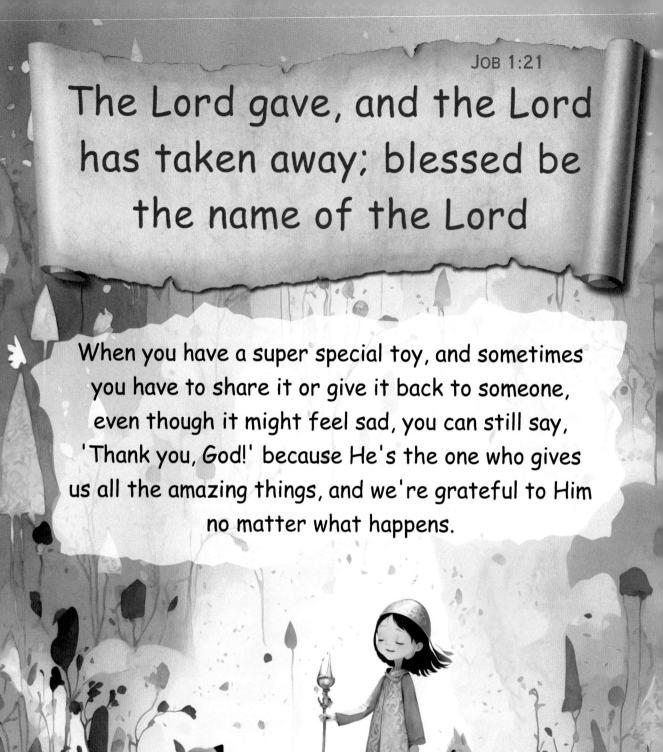

When you have a super special toy, and sometimes you have to share it or give it back to someone, even though it might feel sad, you can still say, 'Thank you, God!' because He's the one who gives us all the amazing things, and we're grateful to Him no matter what happens.

Trust in the Lord with all your heart and lean not on your understanding; in all your ways submit to Him, and He will make your paths straight

Imagine having a magical treasure map, and God is saying, 'Don't just follow what you think is best, trust me with all your heart, let me be your guide, and I'll make sure your journey through life is like a straight and clear path, full of wonderful adventures!'

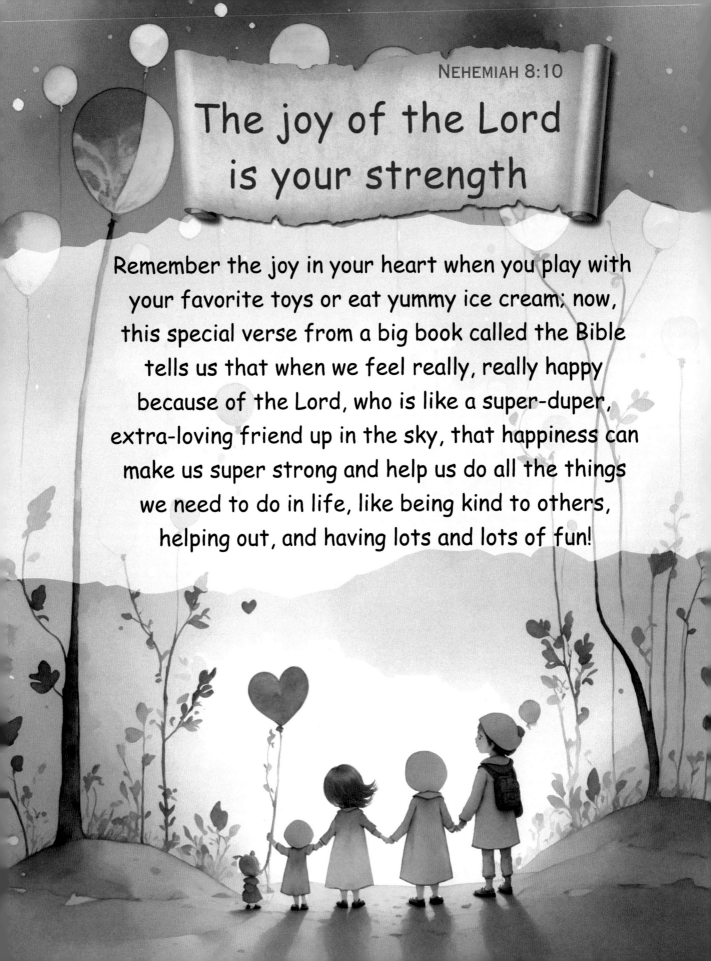

NEHEMIAH 8:10

The joy of the Lord is your strength

Remember the joy in your heart when you play with your favorite toys or eat yummy ice cream; now, this special verse from a big book called the Bible tells us that when we feel really, really happy because of the Lord, who is like a super-duper, extra-loving friend up in the sky, that happiness can make us super strong and help us do all the things we need to do in life, like being kind to others, helping out, and having lots and lots of fun!

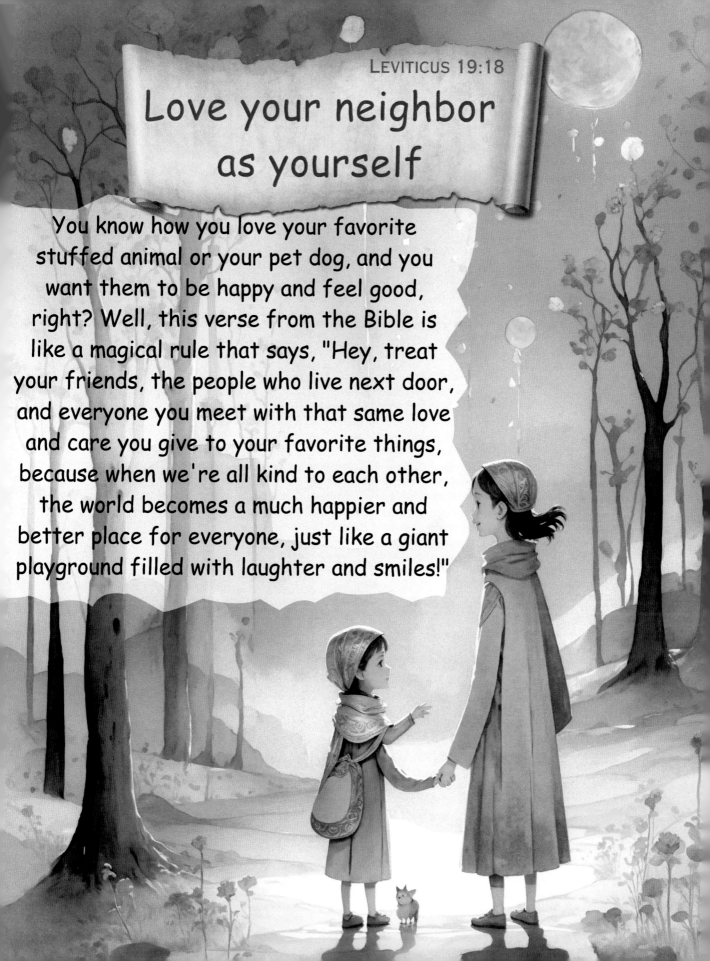

LEVITICUS 19:18

Love your neighbor as yourself

You know how you love your favorite stuffed animal or your pet dog, and you want them to be happy and feel good, right? Well, this verse from the Bible is like a magical rule that says, "Hey, treat your friends, the people who live next door, and everyone you meet with that same love and care you give to your favorite things, because when we're all kind to each other, the world becomes a much happier and better place for everyone, just like a giant playground filled with laughter and smiles!"

DEUTERONOMY 31:6

Be strong and courageous. Do not be afraid or terrified because of them, for the Lord your God goes with you; He will never leave you nor forsake you

Don't worry, don't be scared, even when things seem a bit scary or tough because you have a super-duper, always-there friend, the Lord your God, who sticks by your side through thick and thin, so you can be strong, and you can be as brave as a fearless dragon-slaying hero, because you're never alone!

MATTHEW 7:7

Ask and it will be given to you; seek and you will find; knock and the door will be opened to you

What if you're on a magical quest in a land full of surprises? If you have a big question, if you're looking for something special, or if you want to go on an adventure, all you have to do is ask, look hard, and knock on the doors of opportunity, because when you do, God will help you discover amazing answers, find hidden treasures, and open up new and exciting paths for you to explore!

Man shall not live by bread alone, but by every word that proceeds out of the mouth of God

Imagine your tummy rumbling and you really, really want a yummy sandwich. This special verse is like a wise grown-up saying, "Hey, food is super important, but guess what? It's not just sandwiches and snacks that keep us strong and happy; it's also the kind and loving words from God, like when we hear stories that make us feel warm inside or when we learn how to be good to others, because those words, like magical nourishment for our hearts, help us grow into wonderful people and fill us up with love and goodness!"

Do not store up for yourselves treasures on earth, where moths and vermin destroy,and where thieves break in and steal. But store up for yourselves treasures in heaven, where thieves do not break in.

MATTHEW 6:19-21

Instead of just collecting stuff here on Earth that can disappear or get ruined, try to collect good deeds and acts of kindness, like sharing, being very nice to others, and helping those in need, because those treasures, like golden coins in the sky, stay safe forever, and the more good you do, the more love you'll have in your heart!

But seek first His kingdom and His righteousness, and all these things will be given to you as well

Before you go looking for all the amazing treasures in the world, like shiny toys and delicious treats, first look for ways to be good, like sharing, being kind, and helping others, because when you do that, it's like you're joining a special team with God, and guess what?

God will make sure you have all the good stuff you need, like happiness, love, and everything, because being good and spreading kindness is the greatest treasure of all!

Come to me, all you who are weary and burdened, and I will give you rest

MATTHEW 11:28

You've been running and playing all day, and your little legs are tired... well, this verse from the Bible is like a warm, comforting hug from a kind and gentle friend who says, "Hey, if you're feeling tired and have lots of worries, come to me, and I'll make you feel better, just like when you crawl into your cozy bed after a long, fun day because I'm here to give you rest and make everything feel okay

For where two or three gather in my name, there am I with them

Do you know how when you and your friends get together to play with your toys or have a fun adventure, it feels really special and exciting, right? Well, this verse is like a friendly reminder from God, saying, "Whenever you and even just a couple of your friends gather together to talk about good things and be kind to each other, I'm right there with you, like an invisible superman!"

If we confess our sins, He is faithful and just and will forgive us our sins and purify us from all unrighteousness

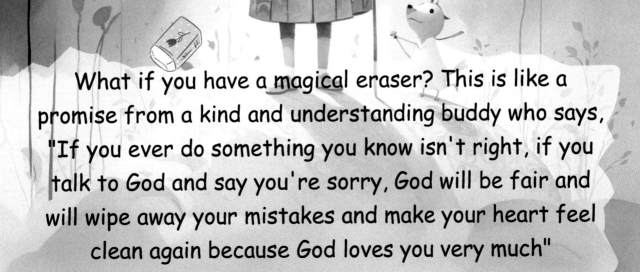

What if you have a magical eraser? This is like a promise from a kind and understanding buddy who says, "If you ever do something you know isn't right, if you talk to God and say you're sorry, God will be fair and will wipe away your mistakes and make your heart feel clean again because God loves you very much"

Yet to all who did receive Him, to those who believed in His name, He gave the right to become children of God

One day you get a special invitation to the most amazing party ever. If you welcome Jesus into your heart, it's like you get a VIP pass to become a part of God's big family, just like brothers and sisters, and that means you're a bright child of God, taking care of you and guiding you through life's adventures!

For God so loved the world that He gave His one and only Son, that whoever believes in Him shall not perish but have eternal life

Let's say you have the most precious toy in the whole wide world. This verse is a declaration from God that says, "I love everyone in the world so much that I shared my most special treasure, my one and only Son, Jesus, with you, and if you believe in Him, it's like getting an amazing, never-ending adventure ticket, where you won't ever have to say goodbye, because you'll have eternal life, like a forever story of love and happiness with God!"

For God did not send His Son into the world to condemn the world, but to save the world through Him

Imagine there's a superhero, and instead of using his powers to punish people, he comes to help them. The promise from God goes like "I didn't send my Son into the world to point fingers or make people feel bad, but rather, I sent Him to be a superhero who saves and loves everyone, like a big, warm hug of goodness, because I want the whole world to find love through my Son, Jesus!"

You have a super bright flashlight, and you get a message from Jesus saying, "If you choose to be my special friend and follow the good and kind things I teach, it's like you have that amazing light with you all the time, and you won't ever feel scared or lost in the dark!""

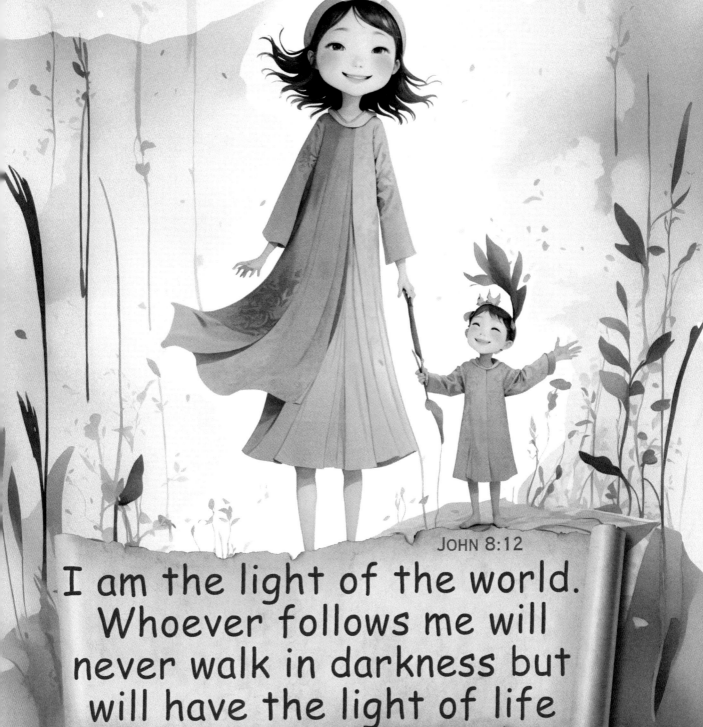

JOHN 8:12

I am the light of the world. Whoever follows me will never walk in darkness but will have the light of life

JOHN 8:32

Then you will know the truth, and the truth will set you free

Today you're on a quest to solve a big mystery, and this verse is a clue that says, "When you search for the truth and understand what's right and good, it's like unlocking a magical door to freedom, where you're not held back by lies or confusion, but you're set free to be the best, happiest, and kindest version of yourself!"

JOHN 10:11

I am the good shepherd. The good shepherd lays down His life for the sheep

Jesus says: "I love you so much that I would even risk my safety to keep you safe and happy, just like how a loving shepherd would protect his sheep from any harm, because you're so precious and dear to me, and I want to make sure you're always taken care of and filled with love!"

JOHN 11:25

I am the resurrection and the life. The one who believes in me will live, even though they die

Jesus says: "I have the power to bring life even to those who have passed away, like waking up from the deepest sleep, because if you believe in me, it's like having a promise of never-ending life, where even when our bodies get tired and old, our spirits will keep on living!"

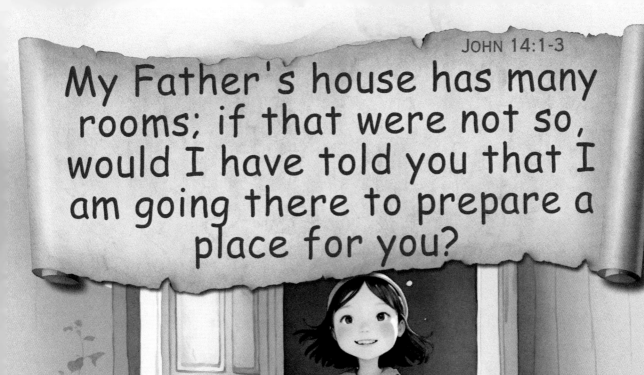

JOHN 14:1-3

My Father's house has many rooms; if that were not so, would I have told you that I am going there to prepare a place for you?

Today you're going on a big journey and Jesus comes along with you saying "Don't be sad or worried, because just like when you visit a friend's house and they have a cozy room waiting for you, I'm getting a wonderful place ready for you in heaven, where you can be with me forever, like a never-ending sleepover with the best friend you could ever have, because I want you to be happy and close to me always!"

I am the vine; you are the branches. If you remain in Me and I in you, you will bear much fruit; apart from Me you can do nothing

You were walking into a park and found a magical tree. There was also Jesus there, saying to you "I'm like the strong and sturdy vine of this tree, and you're like the branches that grow from it, and when you stay connected to me, you can do amazing things and make the world a better place, because without me, it's like trying to make a tree grow without any sunshine or water – it just won't work, but together, we can do great, fruitful things!"

MARK 10:27

With man, this is impossible, but not with God; all things are possible with God

A genie comes at night to you and says "You know, some things may seem really, really hard or even impossible for people to do on their own, like trying to touch the stars or turn invisible, but when you love Jesus, it's like having the ultimate superpower, because He can make even the impossible possible, like a world where dreams come true!"

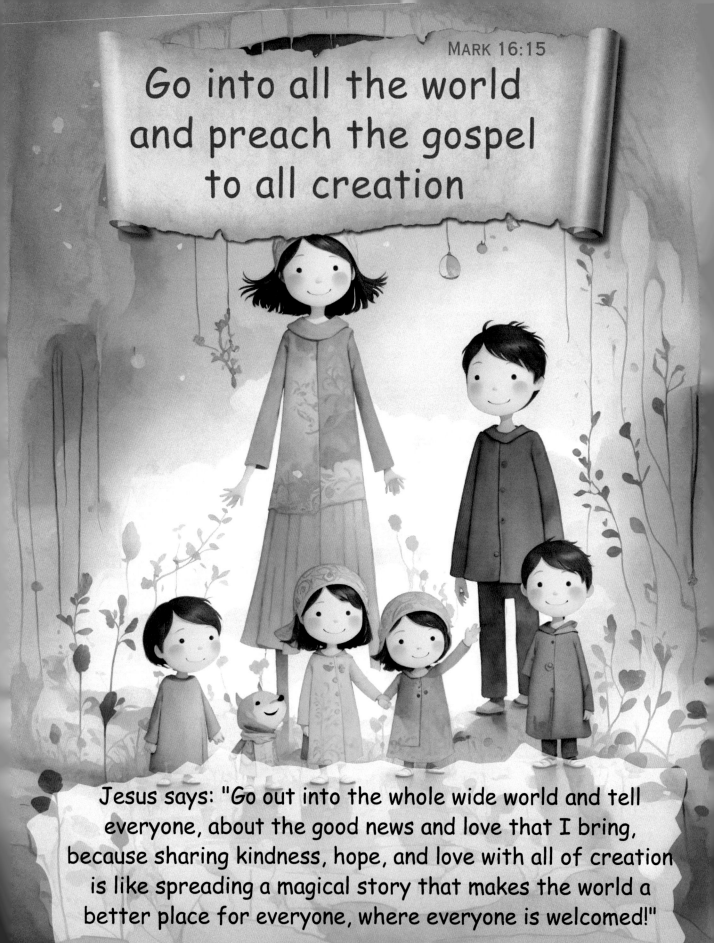

ROMANS 3:23

For all have sinned and fall short of the glory of God

You and your friends are at a park, playing a game, and this verse is like a rule that says, "You know, nobody is perfect; we all make mistakes sometimes, like when you accidentally spill your juice or forget your homework, but that's okay because it's part of being human, and we might not always be as wonderful as God, but that's why we try to learn from our mistakes and be better every day!"

But God demonstrates His own love for us in this: While we were still sinners Christ died for us

Even when we make mistakes and aren't perfect, God loves us so much that he sent His very own son, Jesus, to be like a superhero who gave up His life for us, like a big, warm hug of love that shows us we're never alone, and no matter what, there's always someone who cares for us deeply, just like a never-ending, cozy bedtime story of love and sacrifice.

For the wages of sin is death, but the gift of God is eternal life in Christ Jesus our Lord

When we do things that aren't so good, like telling lies or being mean, it's like earning a sad, not-so-great prize, but God, who's like the most generous gift-giver ever, offers us an amazing present - eternal life with Jesus, like an everlasting party of love and happiness, where we can be close to Him forever!

Do to others as you would have them do to you

LUKE 6:31

Treat everyone the way you want to be treated, like how you'd like your friends to share their toys with you, or how you'd like someone to help when you need it - because when we're kind and to others, it's like making the whole world a happier and more wonderful place, where everyone can be like good friends and spread love and smiles everywhere!

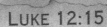

LUKE 12:15

Watch out! Be on your guard against all kinds of greed; life does not consist in an abundance of possessions

Be careful about wanting too many things and being super greedy, because life isn't just about having lots and lots of stuff, like a giant mountain of toys or a huge pile of candy; it's about being happy with what you have and sharing with others, because when we're not too greedy, it's like we find the real treasures of life, like love, friendship, and joy, and that's what makes our hearts the happiest!

JAMES 2:17

In the same way, faith by itself, if it is not accompanied by action, is dead

Having faith is awesome, but it's like having a superpower that's asleep if you don't use it to do good things and be kind to others, because when you combine your faith with actions, like helping someone in need or being a good friend, it's like bringing your wishes to life!

Here I am! I stand at the door and knock. If anyone hears My voice and opens the door, I will come in and eat with that person, and they with Me

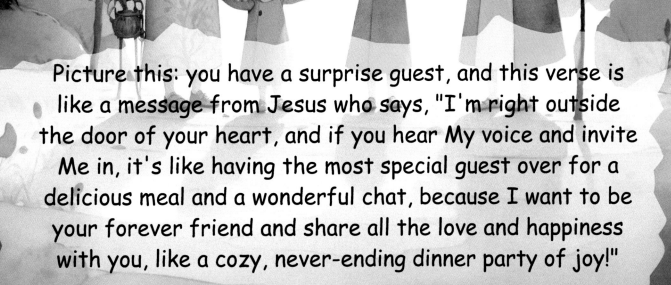

Picture this: you have a surprise guest, and this verse is like a message from Jesus who says, "I'm right outside the door of your heart, and if you hear My voice and invite Me in, it's like having the most special guest over for a delicious meal and a wonderful chat, because I want to be your forever friend and share all the love and happiness with you, like a cozy, never-ending dinner party of joy!"

Whatever you do, work at it with all your heart, as working for the Lord, not for human masters

When you're doing something, like your schoolwork or helping at home, give it your very best, because when you work with all your heart, you spread love and goodness in everything, and it's like making the world a better place!

EPHESIANS 4:32

Be kind and compassionate to one another, forgiving each other, just as in Christ God forgave you

Always be nice and caring to everyone you meet, and if someone makes a mistake, be ready to forgive them, just like how God forgives us when we make mistakes because when we're kind and forgiving, it's like spreading love and happiness all around, making the world a better and happier place for everyone!

TIMOTHY 6:10

For the love of money is a root of all kinds of evil

Loving money more than anything else can lead to doing bad things, like being mean or greedy, but it's important to remember that money isn't the most important thing in the world, and we should treasure things like kindness, love, and being good to others above all else!

CORINTHIANS 13:13

And now these three remain: faith, hope, and love. But the greatest of these is love

In the grand treasure chest of life, there are three super special treasures: **FAITH**, which is believing in wonderful things; **HOPE**, which is looking forward to great things; and **LOVE**, which is the most magical and powerful of all, because when we love each other, it makes the world a truly beautiful and joyful place, and <u>love is the greatest treasure</u> of them all!

Did you liked this book?
If yes, then please tell others so that they can enjoy this amazing book as well!

Want some more?
We have several books already published or coming out soon, so please come back to our store!

Thank you and God bless you!

Pixi Story.com

Made in the USA
Las Vegas, NV
21 October 2023